W9-CHL-542

Going Places

Disney World

Cari Meister

ABDO Publishing Company

visit us at
www.abdopub.com

Published by ABDO Publishing Company 4940 Viking Drive, Edina, Minnesota 55435.
Copyright © 2000 by Abdo Consulting Group, Inc. International copyrights reserved in all
countries. No part of this book may be reproduced in any form without written permission
from the publisher.

Printed in the United States.

Photo credits: Eric Ethan

Edited by Lori Kinstad Pupeza
Contributing editor Morgan Hughes
Graphic designs by Linda O'Leary

Library of Congress Cataloging-in-Publication Data

Meister, Cari.
      Disney World / Cari Meister.
      p. cm. -- (Going Places)
      Includes index.
      Summary: Describes some of the things to see and do at the various parts of Walt
Disney World in Orlando, Florida--the Magic Kingdom, Epcot Center, MGM
Studios, and Disney's Animal Kingdom.
      ISBN 1-57765-025-5
      1. Walt Disney World (Fla.)--Guidebooks--Juvenile literature. 2. EPCOT Center
(Fla.)--Guidebooks--Juvenile literature. 3. Orlando (Fla.)--Guidebooks--Juvenile
literature. [1. Walt Disney World (Fla.)] I. Title. II. Series: Meister, Cari. Going
places.
      GV1853.3.F62D576   2000
      791'.06'875924--dc21   98-9768
                                                             CIP
                                                             AC

Contents

A Magical Place 4

Magic Kingdom: Main Street U.S.A.
  and Adventureland 6

Magic Kingdom: Frontierland, Liberty Square,
  and Fantasyland 8

Magic Kingdom: Tomorrowland and Mickey's
  Toontown Fair 10

Epcot: Future World 12

Epcot: World Showcase 14

Disney-MGM Studios 16

Disney's Animal Kingdom 18

Tips, Tricks, and Other
  Things to Remember 20

Glossary 22

Internet Sites 23

Index 24

A Magical Place

*D*isney World is a magical place. It's a land full of imagination and wonder. Millions of people visit Disney World each year.

Disney World is located in Florida. There are four major theme parks. At the Magic Kingdom, you can meet your favorite Disney characters. You can also ride into fantasy worlds.

At Epcot, you can learn about the future. You can also explore different lands. At Disney-MGM Studios you can act in a movie. You can also watch a real live stunt. At Disney's Animal Kingdom you can see wild animals. You can also take a ride in a **safari** truck.

There are hundreds of other things to do, too. Disney World is always growing. Walt Disney, the man who invented Disney World, wanted new things added every year.

Imagineers are the people who think of new things to add. They are always hard at work.

Florida

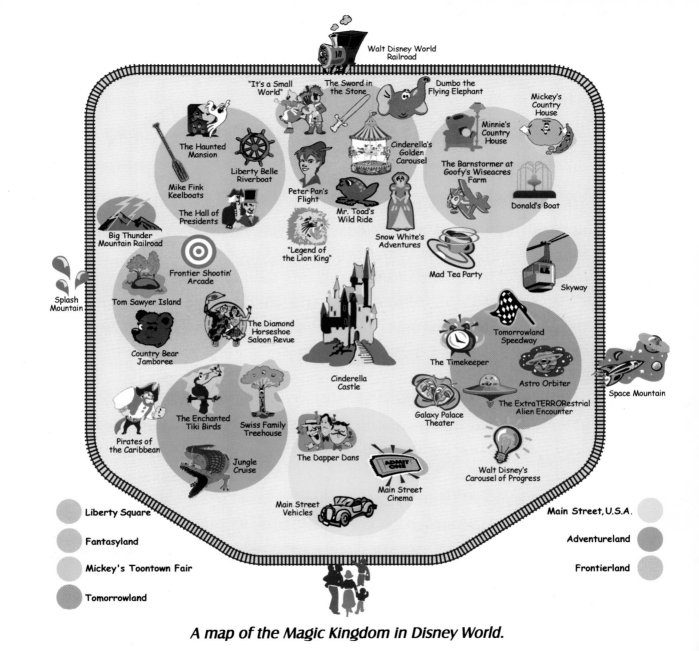

A map of the Magic Kingdom in Disney World.

Walt Disney World Railroad

"It's a Small World"
The Sword in the Stone
Dumbo the Flying Elephant
Mickey's Country House

The Haunted Mansion
Liberty Belle Riverboat
Mike Fink Keelboats
The Hall of Presidents

Minnie's Country House
Cinderella's Golden Carousel
The Barnstormer at Goofy's Wiseacres Farm

Peter Pan's Flight
Mr. Toad's Wild Ride
Snow White's Adventures

Donald's Boat

Big Thunder Mountain Railroad

"Legend of the Lion King"

Mad Tea Party

Frontier Shootin' Arcade

Splash Mountain

Tom Sawyer Island

Skyway

The Diamond Horseshoe Saloon Revue

Country Bear Jamboree

Tomorrowland Speedway

The Timekeeper
Astro Orbiter

Cinderella Castle

The Enchanted Tiki Birds
Swiss Family Treehouse

Galaxy Palace Theater
The ExtraTERRORestrial Alien Encounter

Space Mountain

Pirates of the Caribbean

Jungle Cruise

The Dapper Dans

Main Street Cinema

Walt Disney's Carousel of Progress

Main Street Vehicles

Liberty Square

Fantasyland

Mickey's Toontown Fair

Tomorrowland

Main Street, U.S.A.

Adventureland

Frontierland

Magic Kingdom:
Main Street U.S.A. and Adventureland

The Magic Kingdom is divided into seven lands. They are Main Street U.S.A., Adventureland, Frontierland, Liberty Square, Fantasyland, Tomorrowland, and Mickey's Toontown Fair.

Main Street U.S.A. is like an old town. There are old town shops. You can hear old town music playing. You can ride in a horse-drawn carriage to the end of the street. When you get out, you can see Cinderella's Castle.

Adventureland is just as it sounds. It is a land of adventure! You enter Adventureland by walking over a wooden bridge. Pounding drums, squawking parrots, and the sounds of elephants welcome you.

On the Jungle Cruise, you float through rivers filled with animals. Watch out for Old Smiley the crocodile! Don't worry, he's not real. He only looks real. If you like pirates, jump in line at the Pirates of the Caribbean. Be brave! Your boat will take you through dark caves, loud battles, and past scary skeletons.

Cinderella's Castle.

Magic Kingdom:
Frontierland, Liberty Square, and Fantasyland

*H*ead back in time to the Old West. In Frontierland you will find plenty of cowboy hats and desert bushes. But that's not all. You will also find Disney's most **popular** ride. Be ready to wait. There's always a long line for Splash Mountain. Most people think the ride is worth the wait.

Splash Mountain is a log ride. There are three little dips and one very sharp drop of more than 50 feet (15 m). Warning: you will get wet! Big Thunder Mountain Railroad and Country Bear Jamboree are also in Frontierland.

Learn about American history at Liberty Square. At the Hall of Presidents see **Audio-Animatronics**. They look and sound like real people. Do you like to be scared? Try the Haunted Mansion while you're there.

There are many rides in Fantasyland. Get dizzy in a tea cup at the Mad Tea Party. Fly high in Dumbo, the Flying Elephant. Take a boat ride through It's a Small World. Fly over Neverland in Peter Pan's Flight.

City Hall is part of the Magic Kingdom.

Magic Kingdom:

Tomorrowland and Mickey's Toontown Fair

Don't eat before you go on Space Mountain! Space Mountain is a fast winding roller coaster in Tomorrowland. On this roller coaster, you ride in rocket cars. The rocket cars dash through dark space. Thrilling **special effects** keep you on the edge of your seat.

There are other things to do in Tomorrowland. You can swing through space on the Astro-Orbiter. You can see how life has changed in Carousel of Progress. You can learn about time travel in the Timekeeper.

If you're looking for Mickey Mouse, visit Mickey's Toontown Fair. Mickey is usually walking around. There are other neat things to do here. You can ride in an old airplane at the Barnstormer. You can tour Minnie's country house. You can sit on her couch. You can listen to her messages.

For a surprise, open the refrigerator. Head over to Mickey's Country House when you are done. How do you think the houses will be different?

Tomorrowland shows you the future.

Epcot: Future World

*E*pcot was the second park built at Disney World. Epcot has two parts: Future World and World Showcase.

There are 10 **pavilions** in Future World. You can see Spaceship Earth from anywhere in the park. Spaceship Earth is the big silver building that looks like a golf ball. Spaceship Earth is held up by six posts. They must be very strong because Spaceship Earth weighs over 16 million pounds (7 million kg)! In Spaceship Earth you ride through the history of **communication**. At the end, you are at the top of the ball.

Meet Figment at Journey into Imagination. Figment is a magical creature. He is part lizard, part **steer**, and part crocodile. Inside Journey into Imagination you can walk through a neon tube tunnel. You can step on colors that make sounds. There is also a ride about imagination.

That's just the beginning. Other pavilions feature the ocean, the body, energy, and motion.

The Epcot Center,
Spaceship Earth.

Epcot: World Showcase

*I*magine visiting 11 countries in one day! You can at World Showcase. Each country has its own culture. Try the foods. Listen to the music. Talk to the guides. Even though you're not really in the country, you'll feel like you are.

If you're in a **pyramid**, you're in Mexico. Mexico has a slow and peaceful boat ride. Norway also has a boat ride. The boats have dragon heads. They are meant to look like Viking boats. Watch out for the trolls and the waterfall!

If you are tired, rest in Japan. Japan has peaceful gardens with windchimes and running water. At China, France, and Canada there are movies that you can watch.

In the restaurant in Morocco there's a belly dancer. There's an oompah band in Germany's restaurant. In Italy's restaurant, the waiters sing.

In the United Kingdom, you can see Mary Poppins's street. In the American Adventure, you can visit Ben Franklin and other heroes.

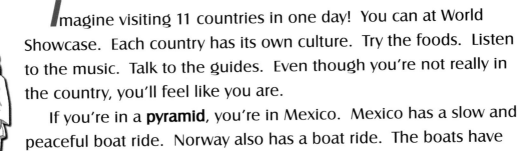

The World Showcase lets you visit many nations; notice a replica of France's Eiffel Tower in the background.

Disney-MGM Studios

*D*id you ever wonder how stunts were done? Did you ever wonder how Disney movies were made?

You can learn all about movie making at Disney-MGM Studios. You might even be able to see the filming of a real movie or TV show.   Disney-MGM Studios is not only a park, but a real **production** center. *Mickey Mouse Club* is filmed there.

Disney-MGM Studios was the third park built at Disney World. There are many fun things to do. You can watch a **3-D** movie with the Muppets. You can see how sounds are made for movies.

At Voyage of the Little Mermaid you can see a live show. You watch the show behind a screen of water. It really seems like you are underwater. You even get wet with sea mist!

Ride a **tram** on the Back Stage Studio Tour. The tram gives you a behind-the-scenes look at costumes, makeup, lighting, and Catastrophe Canyon.

Beauty and the Beast at the Disney-MGM Studios.

17

Disney's Animal Kingdom

*D*isney's Animal Kingdom was the fourth park built at Disney World. It's bigger than all the other parks.

When you enter Animal Kingdom, you will smell flowers. You will feel a light mist. You will see animals. Some animals are real. Other animals are extinct or made-up. The extinct and made-up animals are **models**.

Look for the Tree of Life. The Tree of Life is 14 stories high! The Tree of Life is part of **Safari** Village. At Safari Village you can watch a **3-D** insect film. You can ride in a boat. Keep your eyes open. Monsters pop up from the water.

Do you like dinosaurs? If you do, don't miss Dinoland USA. You can dig up dinosaur bones in the Boneyard.

If you would like to see live animals, go on a Kilimanjaro **Safari**. A guide will drive you in a special safari truck. Hang on! The trucks don't have sides. Watch for elephants, lions, and zebras.

Tips, Tricks, and Other Things to Remember

Disney World is a fun place. It's also very big and crowded. Here are a few tips and tricks to make the most of your visit.

1) Wear comfortable shoes. You will be walking a lot.
2) Plan what you want to see before you come. You will not have time to see everything.
3) Visit the Disney World website for special events and times. www.disneyworld.com
4) Go to the rides with the longest lines first thing in the morning.
5) Eat your meals early to avoid crowds.
6) Wear sunscreen and bring a hat.
7) Don't eat before going on a roller coaster or a spinning ride.
8) Remember that you will spend lots of time waiting in line.

Have fun!

A statue of Walt Disney
and Mickey Mouse.

Glossary

3-D: three dimensional; lifelike.

Audio-animatronics: talking machines that look like people or animals.

Communication: how people talk to each other.

Imagineers: people who work for Disney and think of ideas.

Models: something fake that is made to look like something real.

Pavilion: a building or shelter used in a park.

Popular: favorite.

Production: the process of making something, like a movie.

Pyramid: a giant triangular shaped building.

Safari: a journey to look for animals.

Special effects: special things you hear and see that are added to movies and TV.

Steer: male cattle.

Tram: an overhead boxlike car that runs on a track.

Internet Sites

Canadian CultureNet
http://www.culturenet.ucalgary.ca/
CultureNet is a World Wide Web window on Canadian culture. It is a home for Canadian cultural networks.

The Disney World Explorer
http://www.disney.com/DisneyInteractive/WDWExplorer/
This is a fun and colorful site with trivia games, maps, previews, downloads, CD-ROM helpers and much, much more.

Grand Canyon Association
http://www.thecanyon.com/gca/
You're just a click away from a back-packing trip, a chance to meet canyon lovers like you, and books on this great region. This site has some great artwork.

Mexconnect
http://www.mexconnect.com/
This site has great travel ideas, Mexican art, tradition, food, history, and much more. It includes a chat room, tour section and photo gallery.

Fantastic Journeys Yellowstone
http://www.nationalgeographic.com/features/97/yellowstone/index.html
Explore Yellowstone National Park, a place like no other on Earth. See strange marvels, go underground to find what causes them, and trigger an eruption of the famous geyser Old Faithful. A very cool site!

Marine Watch
http://www.marinewatch.com/
Welcome to Marine Watch, the international news journal about events occuring on, under and over the oceans of the planet. This site has many links and cool photos!

These sites are subject to change.

Pass It On

Adventure Enthusiasts: Tell us about places you've been or want to see. A national park, amusement park, or any exciting place you want to tell us about. We want to hear from you!

To get posted on the ABDO Publishing Company website E-mail us at
"Adventure@abdopub.com"
Visit the ABDO Publsihing Company website at www.abdopub.com

Index

Symbols

3-D movie 16, 18

A

Adventureland 6
American Adventure 14
Animal Kingdom 4, 18
Astro-Orbiter 10

B

Big Thunder Mountain
   Railroad 8

C

Carousel of Progress 10
Cinderella's Castle 6
Country Bear Jamboree 8

D

Dinoland USA 18
dinosaurs 18
Disney characters 4
Disney-MGM 4, 16
Disney, Walt 4, 21

E

Epcot 4, 12, 14

F

Fantasyland 6, 8
Florida 4
Frontierland 6, 8
Future World 12

H

Hall of Presidents 8
Haunted Mansion 8

I

Imagineers 4

J

Journey into Imagination
   12
Jungle Cruise 6

L

Liberty Square 6, 8

M

Magic Kingdom 4, 6,
   8, 10
Main Street U.S.A. 6
Mickey Mouse 10, 21
Mickey Mouse Club 16
Mickey's Toontown Fair
   6, 10

monsters 18
Muppets 16

O

Old Smiley the crocodile
   6

P

Pirates of the Caribbean
   6

S

safari 4, 18
Safari Village 18
Space Mountain 10
Spaceship Earth 12
special effects 10
Splash Mountain 8

T

theme park 4
Tomorrowland 6, 10
Tree of Life 18

V

Voyage of the Little
   Mermaid 16

W

World Showcase 12, 14